Sophie

"How can the End
be the Beginning again
when All seems Lost?"

A One-Act Play
based on the Writings
of Sophie Large
by
Bryan Willis.

Illustrations
by
Sophie Large.

Sophie by Bryan Willis – © 2002

**This play was commissioned by Sophie's Silver Lining Fund, U.K. Registered Charity No. 1071883.
Additional funding provided by Rain City Projects, Seattle, WA, U.S.A.**

Designed and printed by Rosy Burke Design Associates Ltd.
19 Banbury Road, Chacombe, Banbury, Oxfordshire OX17 2JN, England.

Special thanks to all of the people who contributed their time and devotion to this project: Erin Hurme, Samm Line,
Giles Ramsay, Richard Demarco, O.B.E., Richard Bridgland, Sally Foord-Kelcey, Amy May Bowes, Alex Dobson, Rosy Burke,
Bruce Smith, Philippa Foord-Kelcey, Nina Wilson, Bret Fetzer and the Board of Rain City Projects, M. Burke Walker,
John Pumphrey, David Haig, Nadine Mills, Edward Dick, Victoria Hart, Stephen Kelsey, Jo Clarke, Hannah Kappler,
Chris & Wendy Hart, Bill & Margaret Hurme, Susan Willis, Joyce Smith, St. Swithun's School, June Ringe, Linda Wollen,
Maggie Hunter, Tim Johnson, Charlotte Tiencken, Terry Ann Newman, Sir Andrew Large, Tony Scott-Andrews,
Tracy Huddleson, Peter Hurme, Ed Trotter and Edward Kemp.

The play could not have been written without the support of Sophie's remarkable family.
Grateful acknowledgement is made to Sophie's brothers, Jeremy and Oliver, as well as her parents, Cherry and Stephen.

*Patron: Dame
Judi Dench*

Sophie's Silver Lining Fund
which supports needy acting and singing students
was officially formed into a
UK Registered Charity in October 1998.
Registered Charity Number: 1071883.
Registered address: 17 Silver Street, Chacombe,
Banbury, Oxon, OX17 2JR, England.

Patron: Dame Judi Dench.
Trustees: Cherry and Stephen Large, Sir Andrew Large,
David Haig, Sally Foord-Kelcey and Tony Scott-Andrews.

Detailed information about the Fund and its activities
can be found by visiting the Charity's Website at

www.silverlining.org.uk

For Cherry

~ This book within doth stories tell, ~
~ Of fairies witches, Hea'n and Hell, ~
~ Read on, my friend, enjoy my book, ~
~ I prithee now to take a look. ~

~ God bless you, sir, madame, miss, ~
~ which ever title bring you bliss, ~
~ enjoy these stories, when they're writ, ~
~ 'Till Then you'll have to wait a bit. ~

It is with life as with a play—
it matters not how long the
action is spun out, but how
good the acting is.

Seneca

What made us dream that he could comb grey hair?

William Butler Yeats,
In Memory of
Major Robert Gregory

Extracts from Sophie's Log *

On being alone at a railway station

A strange grey town
Blotted out by night;
Deep voids of crowded air,
A flickering neon sign,
A deserted platform.
Across the other side,
On red benches no-one sits.
The box clock ticks, echoes
In the brimming space.
Flick, a minute passes.

But more –
People hurry to rain flecked cars
Enclosed in metal,
Relieved and going home.
An image of evening –
Television, warmth, food.
People beyond yellow squares,
Who see no rivulet stranger.
A barrier of space makes her
Untouchable.
(Sitting in the dust, fierce sun,
Fire wounds sweet smelling death).

And more –
People drain away to duvets
The streets, full of no-one,
Transform.
As her tired footsteps pass,
Blank building faces
Are dispassionate judges.
Under their gaze, people
Draw in, shiver, scurry
To bolt holes, protection.
Hurry in the hostile air.
Night streets are no place for people.

And more.
Yellow black clouds
Blanket thick, sinking
Sludge on the station.
And trains, vast heaves
Of agonising noise –
A flicker of faces, coffee cups,
Framed by black –
Flick flick flick swoosh
Gone. Wind in her fingers.
The dark resignation hunches.
There are no trains stop here tonight.

By Sophie, aged eighteen.

Catkins

Catkins, hanging in the sun,
Pollen enough for everyone,
Will you still hang there when I'm gone,
When your job is done?

I wish I were like you, small and light,
When I die I think I might
Soar and fly through the night,
'Till my job is done.

By Sophie, aged eleven.

** Sophie's Log – thoughts
and feelings in poetry
and prose by
Sophie Large.
ISBN 0-9534901-0-6
from Ottakar's Bookshop
in England.
Tel: +44 (0) 1295 270498.
Or from www.wheesh.com*

Tori Hart and Erin Hurme as Young Sophie and Sophie at Edinburgh Festival Fringe 2002.
Photo: Clive Barda.

Sophie premiered 5 August 2002
at the Edinburgh Festival Fringe.
Produced by Richard Demarco, O.B.E.
and Rocket Productions.
Directed by Giles Ramsay.
Set by Richard Bridgland.
Stage Managers were Samm Line and Oliver Large.
Photos by Clive Barda.
The poem *Catkins* was recorded by Jenny Agutter.
Cast:
Sophie – Erin Hurme
Young Sophie – Tori Hart

In October 2003 a workshop production was staged
by the Westside Theater Company at the
Mariah Art School in Olympia, Washington, USA.
Directed by John Ficker.
Set by Richard Bridgland.
Katy Fogg was the Stage Manager.
Cast:
Sophie – Heidi Rider
Young Sophie – Kaille Kirkham

Sophie

The young Sophie

Cast:

Young Sophie aged 13 – *An intellectual Tigger.*
Questions, questions, questions.
Sophie aged 19 – *Currently on her gap year.*
Directing a play scheduled to premiere at
the Edinburgh Festival Fringe.
Time – February 1998.
Set – A bench on the platform of an outdoor railway station.
Running Time – 50 minutes.

Sophie, aged 18

SFX of a commuter train passing through a station. Flickering light and shadows play upon the face of YOUNG SOPHIE, who sits on a red bench, a small travel bag by her side. The Sound fades–the lights of the station and early evening illuminate the scene. YOUNG SOPHIE opens a bag of crisps and addresses the audience.

YOUNG SOPHIE My Ten Wishes. The first ones I call *Helpful Wishes*: No more wars or pollution and I would wish for the weather to behave itself. I wish it would rain just enough for agricultural uses – and only at night. I wish for the ground to become fertile in non-fertile countries.

And now for the exciting ones: I wish I could talk to animals and breathe under water. I wish I could ride really well and become small whenever required. I wish I could fly . . . Are you counting? I hope not. I wish my dad to be sent one million pounds – but don't tell him I said so.

Train sound/SFX.

I have one more wish, an incredibly important one; I'll give you three seconds to guess what it is!

SOPHIE enters without a bag or winter coat. She looks a bit disoriented.

SOPHIE Was that the train to Middleton?!

YOUNG SOPHIE Sorry!

SOPHIE The train that just passed. Was it going to Middleton?

YOUNG SOPHIE Oh, I wasn't looking, sorry. I suppose it's possible.

SOPHIE Are you –

YOUNG SOPHIE I'm going to Fellbridge. Sorry, I –

SOPHIE No, I was going to –

YOUNG SOPHIE Actually, I'm not the right person to ask. You see, this isn't my station. I got off thinking this was Fellbridge.

SOPHIE *(Amused.)* Fellbridge? I should think not.

YOUNG SOPHIE My mistake.

SOPHIE *(Still amused.)* This doesn't look the slightest bit like Fellbridge.

YOUNG SOPHIE Then I suppose you know exactly where you are?

SOPHIE Yes, I was just – I. *(Looks around.)* You'd think there'd be a sign some-where.

YOUNG SOPHIE You'd think so.

SOPHIE And the ticket office?

YOUNG SOPHIE There's no one there. If I'm not mistaken, it closed just as I arrived.

SOPHIE And when was that?

YOUNG SOPHIE Two hours ago.

SOPHIE My God.

YOUNG SOPHIE I don't mind. By my calculations, the next train to Fellbridge should be here . . . any moment. Of course –

SOPHIE Yes –

YOUNG SOPHIE It would help if I knew where we were. *(To an unseen pres-ence/Audience.)* I CAN MANAGE PERFECTLY WELL ON MY OWN, THANK YOU!

SOPHIE Sorry?

YOUNG SOPHIE That bloke over there. *(To the unseen presence/Audience.)* I'M FINE, REALLY. DON'T BE SUCH A PEST.

SOPHIE That bloke over –

YOUNG SOPHIE The odd fellow lurking about.

SOPHIE I'm afraid I don't –

YOUNG SOPHIE *(To the presence/Audience:)* NO. CRISPS.

SOPHIE I really don't –

YOUNG SOPHIE I know he looks a bit scary, but he's not entirely bad. If you must know, sometimes he keeps me company. When there's no one else to talk to.

SOPHIE . . . Oh. I see. *(Waves to the imaginary friend.)* Hello! *(To YOUNG SOPHIE.)* He's not the least bit scary. In fact, he's rather – dashing, don't you think?

YOUNG SOPHIE I think he's after my crisps . . . Don't look. Maybe he'll go away.

They look away.

SOPHIE Would you mind terribly if I sit?

YOUNG SOPHIE Please.

SOPHIE joins YOUNG SOPHIE on the bench.

YOUNG SOPHIE . . . Crisps?

SOPHIE Thank you, no. Actually –

YOUNG SOPHIE *(Tempting.)* Smoky Bacon.

SOPHIE I think I'll just ring my mum.

YOUNG SOPHIE Right. There's a call box down the platform.

SOPHIE Would you like to come with me?

YOUNG SOPHIE I'll be fine.

SOPHIE You're positive?

YOUNG SOPHIE Absolutely.

SOPHIE I'll keep a close watch.

YOUNG SOPHIE Thank you. Last call for crisps.

SOPHIE Well then. *(Takes some.)* Thanks.

They smile. SOPHIE exits.

YOUNG SOPHIE *(Takes the final crisps, folds the empty bag and addresses the Audience.)* There's no need to rush, you know. Really, when it's time to go, we'll go. That's part of growing up, isn't it. Knowing you can't control every little thing. *(Returns the crisps bag to her satchel.)* Did you know you were in my dreams last night? I tossed and turned in bed. I think I dozed, then I woke to find my room flooded with silver light. I got out of bed and at the window I saw a shape appear over the horizon of the moon: a horse. Yes, a horse with silver wings. I promise it, I'm not fibbing, it was a horse. It came over to my room and we climbed on his back and sawed through the air. Every now and then he glanced at the moon – his home.

SOPHIE returns and listens to YOUNG SOPHIE.

I thought it was a dream but my legs are covered in moon dust. Will she believe me? Noo.

SOPHIE Will she believe what?

YOUNG SOPHIE . . . Last night I flew to the moon on a silver horse.

SOPHIE Ohh, that explains it.

YOUNG SOPHIE What?

SOPHIE The moon dust on your shoes. I was wondering how that got there.

They both watch as another train passes accompanied by the distant sound of a police siren and ambulance. SFX. They may speak with voices raised as the sounds tail off.

SOPHIE I have an incredible favour to ask! It's just a tiny bit embarrassing!

YOUNG SOPHIE Are you all right?! You look a bit – peaked!

SOPHIE I'm fine, really! I-I don't know what I did with my bag!

YOUNG SOPHIE You didn't have it when you arrived!

The train is well past.

SOPHIE That's right I-I'm not sure where it is and I – don't seem to have any money. Absolutely nothing.

YOUNG SOPHIE The phone.

SOPHIE Yes.

YOUNG SOPHIE I have 10p in my belt.

SOPHIE Fantastic.

YOUNG SOPHIE *(Looks at her waist – the belt is missing.)*
It's in my satchel. Hang on.

SOPHIE If it's not too much of a bother.

YOUNG SOPHIE *(Pulling stuff out of her bag: parts of a school uniform, a toy badger, which she tries to cover. She also tries to conceal some bulky, brown institutional shorts.)*
I know it's in here somewhere.

SOPHIE Is it Edmund's College then?

YOUNG SOPHIE Is it that obvious?

SOPHIE You said Fellbridge. And then there's the uniform.

YOUNG SOPHIE Right.

SOPHIE And those hideous brown knickers.

YOUNG SOPHIE Aren't they awful? Honestly, I can't think of one nice thing to say about them. Except perhaps they're bulletproof. At least that's the rumour.

SOPHIE Lucy Spencer burned hers the minute she left.

YOUNG SOPHIE *(Finds the 10p.)* Then I take it you went to Edmund's?

SOPHIE Not a very encouraging sign, is it.

YOUNG SOPHIE Sorry?

SOPHIE A fellow old girl. A recent leaver and here I am borrowing 10p at a railway station.

YOUNG SOPHIE Go on.

SOPHIE I don't want to clear you out.

YOUNG SOPHIE *(Whispers:)* Don't worry. I have more.

Ode to waiting for a Call.

Oh my heart weeps
Oh my soul is stone
As I sit sobbing
By the Telephone
I plead and cry and beg
The plastic telephone
But it is no use
No matter how I moan)
For sadly, sadly,

SOPHIE *(Whispers back.)* Okay. Thanks.

Sophie

YOUNG SOPHIE *(More whispering.)* My pleasure. By the way, my name's Sophie.

SOPHIE *(It's a whisper fest.)* Oh my god, we're walking cliches!

YOUNG SOPHIE Are you Sophie –

SOPHIE I am. Though officially it's Sophia *(So-fi-uh)*.

YOUNG SOPHIE Me too!

SOPHIA C. A. LARGE

SOPHIE *(As she exits.)* Brilliant. Thanks so much. Scream if you need me.

YOUNG SOPHIE *(To the Audience.)* Honestly, I'm not altogether sure she's ready, do you? I should tell her none of the phones work, but she would still give it a go. That's one of the problems of being my age: No one believes you. Except other children, but they don't interest me much. I do enjoy small children. And adults of all ages. Sometimes I wish I could just skip childhood altogether and go straight to being an adult. Not that I'm in such a hurry. Believe me.

I got into a real mess today because I looked at some old photos of Mummy and Daddy. They really affected me. I think it's the idea of time running away, and seeing children – carefree children – on paper before you, and the old adults next to them. I could hardly get over it. I burst into tears and Tilly, dearest Tilly licked my face and seemed to understand and I just sat there for ages crying.

Dearest Parents,

It's the idea of so many days gone that were wasted or that I don't remember. Each second moving and never there again; and that some day Mum and Dad will die, and some day I'll die; it's years away, but quick as a flash those years'll be gone and all that will be left of them is a pile of old photos. I know there's more to it than that, but still –

SFX: TRAIN; SOPHIE returns in a rush.

SOPHIE I thought that might be ours! Who were you –

YOUNG SOPHIE *(To the presence/Audience.)* I think it's okay if you want to say hello! This is my friend Sophie.

SOPHIE *(To the presence/Audience.)* Hello?

YOUNG SOPHIE . . . The truth is he's actually quite shy.

SOPHIE *(To the presence/Audience.)* Hello. I'm Sophie.

YOUNG SOPHIE . . . Did you reach your Mum?

SOPHIE No. And the connection was a bit odd. I wasn't able to reach a soul. Including the operator.

YOUNG SOPHIE I can't say I'm surprised.

SOPHIE Were you able to reach anyone? Your mum?

YOUNG SOPHIE No, I'm afraid not; they've all gone. There's been an accident.

SOPHIE Was it just around – was it that blue car and the lorry?

YOUNG SOPHIE Yes, it was just over –

SOPHIE Oh my god, I think I saw that. Is everyone all right?

YOUNG SOPHIE Actually – no. But they will be.

SOPHIE Nothing too serious I hope.

YOUNG SOPHIE They'll be all right.

SOPHIE Good. That's reassuring. I – I just don't recognize anything.

YOUNG SOPHIE Sorry?

SOPHIE Does anything look familiar?

YOUNG SOPHIE To me? This station?

SOPHIE If it's close to the school you'd think we'd recognize something. Don't you?

YOUNG SOPHIE I usually get a lift from my parents. It's just today, with the (accident) –

SOPHIE Right.

YOUNG SOPHIE I don't want to admit it, but I fell asleep. Obviously I passed my station. *(To the presence/Audience.)* AND THANK YOU SO MUCH FOR THE WARNING. *(To SOPHIE.)* He's not shy, he's ashamed.

SOPHIE So the next train that stops should go back towards Fellbridge.

YOUNG SOPHIE Exactly.

SOPHIE Right.

A moment.

SOPHIE Here's your 10p. Thanks.

YOUNG SOPHIE Please keep it.

SOPHIE Nonsense. This belongs in your – Is that a Badger?!

YOUNG SOPHIE No, it's uh, actually it's a hat.

SOPHIE *(She pulls out the badger – a small book falls out of the bag.)* I still have my Badger; of course he's not quite as fuzzy as –

YOUNG SOPHIE Ohmygod-don't-look.

A moment. SOPHIE looks away.

SOPHIE Shall I pick it up then?

YOUNG SOPHIE Did you see it?

SOPHIE If you mean, "Did you see the big pink letters on the cover that read "*Snog List*", I'm afraid I must say yes.

YOUNG SOPHIE Ohmygod. No one's ever seen that, I would rather lick tar off the road than have anyone read so much as one page of that book.

SOPHIE My goodness, how many boys have you snogged?

YOUNG SOPHIE Oh, you know. The usual number.

SOPHIE It's nothing to be ashamed about.

YOUNG SOPHIE Of course not.

SOPHIE *(Returns the Snog List to the bag.)* I'm sure no one would read it without your permission. I know I wouldn't.

YOUNG SOPHIE Can I ask you a personal question?

SOPHIE laughs.

YOUNG SOPHIE I'm quite serious.

SOPHIE Yes. Of course.

YOUNG SOPHIE . . . How many boys had you snogged by the time you were, say, thirteen. And a half.

SOPHIE Thirteen. Hmm. Let me think.

YOUNG SOPHIE I met a really nice boy last week. I mean really nice. He's pleasant looking and has beautiful puppy dog eyes. He was really nice to me and I had a heart to heart with him and touched on subjects I find really interesting – infinity, stuff like that. He plays guitar and I sang along to his playing and it felt so –

SOPHIE Right.

YOUNG SOPHIE Yes. I mean, we seemed to hit it off really well.

SOPHIE And you don't want to rush it?

YOUNG SOPHIE I don't! That's the thing, I have to be careful. I've only known him for about 74 hours. Which is long enough to know I think he's one of the nicest people I've ever met. Also long enough to know he's not on the pull. He's too genuine and faithful to snog anyone while he fancies this one girl from home.

SOPHIE Annoying, isn't it.

YOUNG SOPHIE Sorry.

SOPHIE "The Girl from Home".

YOUNG SOPHIE It's not, really. Not when you remember girlfriend-boyfriend relationships don't last long, do they? It's a lot maturer to be able to like someone and be good friends. I mean, say, if as soon as you start liking a boy, you snog him, you know each other too well physically, but not well enough mentally, and more often than not the whole thing falls through. And that's why I decided on a definite course of action with this boy. Would you like to hear my plan?

SOPHIE If I said *No* would you hate me forever.

YOUNG SOPHIE (*About to burst.*) Yes. I'd like to meet him socially a few times. Forget Romance. Don't Tell anyone I Like Him. And then see how things progress. Naturally. Because the other thing is that he's so nice to everyone, not just me. He treated me the same as everyone else, perhaps with a teeny bit more reserve because he doesn't know me as well as most of the others. So it goes to show he doesn't fancy me. And for that I'm glad. So if anything happens it'll be based on friendship and mutual interests. But I'd value him, his friendship, so much right now. So I must, at all costs, I must Keep It To Myself.

SOPHIE . . . What.

YOUNG SOPHIE Keep it to myself. The fact that I fancy this boy.

SOPHIE Keep what to yourself?

YOUNG SOPHIE The *Secret* that I – ha ha.

SOPHIE That wasn't very polite of me. Sorry.

YOUNG SOPHIE To be perfectly honest? This is empty. I haven't snogged anyone.

SOPHIE There's no rush.

YOUNG SOPHIE I don't know what's worse – to be my age and have a *Snog List* positively bulging with juicy entries, or to have nothing at all. All the pages, perfectly blank.
She looks at SOPHIE . . . bursts into tears. SOPHIE puts an arm around YOUNG SOPHIE's shoulders.

SOPHIE . . . I have a good joke if you'd like to hear it.

YOUNG SOPHIE *(Wipes away a snuffle.)* Thank you.

SOPHIE Knock-knock.

YOUNG SOPHIE Who's there?

SOPHIE Interrupting Cow.

YOUNG SOPHIE Interrupting Cow Who –

SOPHIE *(Interrupting.)* MOOOOOOOOOO!

A moment. Udder silence.

YOUNG SOPHIE I've got one, but it's not as funny as that.

SOPHIE Well then, by all means.

YOUNG SOPHIE No, seriously. It's not particularly good.

SOPHIE Come on, how bad could it be?

YOUNG SOPHIE It's dreadful. Even my brothers hate it.

SOPHIE Now I really must hear it.

YOUNG SOPHIE It's a better joke than I can tell it. I'm still working on the timing.

SOPHIE Is the actual joke as long as your explanation as to why it's not a good joke?

YOUNG SOPHIE . . . No.

SOPHIE Then let's hear it.

YOUNG SOPHIE Right. Okay. Why did the squirrel fall out of the tree? *(Sotto to SOPHIE:)* I don't know, why did –

SOPHIE I don't know, why *did* the squirrel fall out of the tree?

YOUNG SOPHIE Because he was dead. Why did the second squirrel fall out of the tree?

SOPHIE I don't know, why *did* the second squirrel fall out of the tree?

YOUNG SOPHIE Because he was stapled to the chicken – stapled to the other squirrel. Why did the third chicken –

SOPHIE Squirrel?

YOUNG SOPHIE Squirrel, sorry. Why did the third squirrel fall out of the tree?

SOPHIE I don't know, why *did* the third squirrel fall out of the tree?

YOUNG SOPHIE Because he thought it was trendy. Why did the tree fall over?

SOPHIE I don't know, why *did* the tree fall over?

YOUNG SOPHIE Because he thought he was a squirrel. The End . . . Why aren't you laughing?

SOPHIE I'm smiling.

YOUNG SOPHIE It's not very good, is it?

SOPHIE I wasn't sure about that bit with the chicken.

YOUNG SOPHIE That was a mistake. There are no chickens in that joke. Not when you tell it correctly.

SOPHIE   Oh.

SOPHIE laughs.

YOUNG SOPHIE   You're just being nice.

SOPHIE   No, that's-that's funny. Really. Now if you don't mind, I'm going to try my mum again.

YOUNG SOPHIE   You'll need the 10p.

SOPHIE   That's so kind, but –

YOUNG SOPHIE   It's right here. I can give you more if you need it.

SOPHIE   I'll try reversing the charges. They'll understand.

YOUNG SOPHIE   I'm sure they will.

SOPHIE   Wish me luck.

YOUNG SOPHIE   Luck.

SOPHIE exits.

YOUNG SOPHIE quite deliberately places a large book on the bench. Now she moves away as we hear the Sound of a Train approaching.

YOUNG SOPHIE drums her hands on her thigh to the rhythm of the train. SOPHIE rushes in.

SOPHIE   That's the one! Come on, we'll stop it ourselves if we have to! Will you help me flag it down?! Sophie! *(Laughs. Calls to the train:)* HELLO! We're here! We're cold! We're all set to go! *(Looks to YOUNG SOPHIE on the bench. Laughs.)* I'm all set to go! *(To YOUNG SOPHIE:)* Come on! *(To the passing Train:)* We're here! We're . . . here. We're . . . Damn . . . WE'RE STILL WAITING! . . . Sorry.

YOUNG SOPHIE   It can be frustrating.

SOPHIE   And if it does stop I haven't got any money. My God –

YOUNG SOPHIE   That won't be a problem.

SOPHIE   You're sure. That's very kind.

YOUNG SOPHIE   I'm happy to help, really.

SOPHIE I had a satchel and at least five quid. No, it was – honestly, I can't remember.

YOUNG SOPHIE It's all right.

SOPHIE I was in the car. I was driving.

YOUNG SOPHIE Of course you were.

SOPHIE My satchel was right beside me and I didn't stop. But I must have. *(Laughs.)*

YOUNG SOPHIE *(Gives SOPHIE a jumper.)* Sophie.

SOPHIE I've got myself all confused.

YOUNG SOPHIE Well you're here now.

SOPHIE *(Putting on jumper.)* Right. Thank you. *(Sees the book.)* Am I keeping you from your studies?

YOUNG SOPHIE Ohh, that's not a school book, it's – oh it's silly.

SOPHIE It's a book about Flower Fairies.

YOUNG SOPHIE Well I'm, you know, I'm, I'm –

SOPHIE Yes.

YOUNG SOPHIE I'm much too old for that sort of thing –

SOPHIE Nonsense.

YOUNG SOPHIE I am! But they're read all over England.

SOPHIE Mm-hmn.

YOUNG SOPHIE It's true. And they're very popular with little girls. So I thought I'd read this book and.

SOPHIE And?

YOUNG SOPHIE Then try to write some. Fairy poems. To sell.

SOPHIE So you don't believe in them yourself?

YOUNG SOPHIE Believe in what?

SOPHIE Flower fairies.

YOUNG SOPHIE Of course not.

SOPHIE Because you know I do.

YOUNG SOPHIE That's because you're a Drama Queen.

SOPHIE *(Finds this last comment highly amusing.)* How old are you?

YOUNG SOPHIE Too old for flower fairy poems.

SOPHIE Right. Then I suppose it would be a waste of time to ask you to make one up with me.

A moment.

SOPHIE Beneath the bracken
　　By the stream.
　　Lives a pixie
　　Decked in . . . .

YOUNG SOPHIE . . . Green.

SOPHIE A word! Bing-bing-bing! We have a winner! Of course, I recognize you're far too mature to offer any further collaborative –

YOUNG SOPHIE Her wings are clear
　　As clear can be.

SOPHIE I thought pixies were usually male.

YOUNG SOPHIE Not this one.

SOPHIE Sorry. Her wings are –

YOUNG SOPHIE Clear
　　As clear can be.

SOPHIE And none can see him – her.

SOPHIE & **YOUNG SOPHIE** Only me.

SOPHIE Beside the oak tree
　　In the roots,
　　Lives an elf
　　With mouse-skin

SOPHIE & YOUNG SOPHIE Boots.

SOPHIE He plays the pipe

YOUNG SOPHIE Just like a bird

SOPHIE By me alone

SOPHIE & YOUNG SOPHIE His song is heard.

SOPHIE 'Neath the –

YOUNG SOPHIE Rose bush.

SOPHIE Blooming wild,
  Is a lovely –

YOUNG SOPHIE Fairy child.
  The fragrance of the bush
  Is she.

SOPHIE But no one knows this.

YOUNG SOPHIE Only me.

SOPHIE Within the waters
  Of the brook,
  Lives a – lives a

YOUNG SOPHIE Water nymph?
  In a – nook.

SOPHIE Hmm.

YOUNG SOPHIE A bit awkward, that.

SOPHIE 'Tis she that makes the waters
shine.

YOUNG SOPHIE But this knowledge . . . .

SOPHIE & YOUNG SOPHIE Is only mine.

SOPHIE And so, my children,
  Hear my tale.

YOUNG SOPHIE The gift of magic will –

SOPHIE Prevail.
   Within your minds,
   You alone can see.

YOUNG SOPHIE The elf who lives.

YOUNG SOPHIE & SOPHIE Beneath the
   tree.

SOPHIE Very nice.

YOUNG SOPHIE Thank you.

SOPHIE Of course you'll give me half credit and a generous royalty.

YOUNG SOPHIE Of course.

SOPHIE And there's something else you'll have to explain to me.

YOUNG SOPHIE Yes?

SOPHIE Why is it – you see, I've never seen flower fairy books with full colour
fashion shots of all my favorite celebs –

*She lunges for the fairy book. A struggle ensues – it's all fun and giggles. SOPHIE pulls
out a glitzy teen magazine from inside the facade of the flower fairy book.*

YOUNG SOPHIE It's not what you think. Nooo!

SOPHIE Let's see, something's marked here – I wonder – THE ADVICE PAGE?!

More laughter as YOUNG SOPHIE eventually wins the battle for her teen magazine.

YOUNG SOPHIE Did you have any luck with your mum?

SOPHIE All the phones have gone dead. Honestly, I couldn't get so much as a
dialing tone from any of them.

YOUNG SOPHIE Imagine that.

SOPHIE Yes.

YOUNG SOPHIE I want some crisps. Would you like some?

SOPHIE I really am trying to cut down on my in-betweens.

YOUNG SOPHIE *(Tempting.)* Cheesy Onion.

SOPHIE   Oh, if I must.

YOUNG SOPHIE   I'm going to start a diet next week. I'm going to find out how much I weigh and by the end of term, I'm going to weigh less.

SOPHIE   As long as it's reasonable.

YOUNG SOPHIE   Absolutely. I have exams, so I can't be expected to diet seriously. But I can be expected to cut down in easy ways. I'm just so tired of being fed up with my figure. So. More Exercise. Cut down on my in-betweens. I'm going to make a schedule and stick to it.

SOPHIE *(Etiquette Breach – as she's munching.)* Absolutely.

YOUNG SOPHIE   Do you think my hyper-organization will last much past tomorrow?

SOPHIE *(Indicates her mouth is full.)* Ummmm.

YOUNG SOPHIE   The funny thing is, well not funny, but the truth of the matter is it's not a problem at home. It's –

SOPHIE   It's school.

YOUNG SOPHIE   It is.

SOPHIE   May I?

YOUNG SOPHIE *(Hands the bag to SOPHIE.)* At home, I feel much happier. I can't work out why. Maybe because in many ways you're much more alone at school. You can't turn to someone because they think you're attention seeking or being pathetic. So you bottle it up or avoid people. I'm never totally happy there. I'm always niggling at myself. Not other people, myself. And I'm happy with my internal self. It's my *outside*. My squished up bumpy face and limp hair and big bum and stomach. My flat feet. I look in my mirror and I see – A pear. A giant pear with big feet. And hands. I hate my hands.

SOPHIE *(Folds the empty bag with the exact gesture used earlier by YOUNG SOPHIE.)* I hate my hands. I always have. But yours –

YOUNG SOPHIE   You have beautiful hands.

SOPHIE Oh yes, particularly with the bits of crisps stuck under the nails. Lovely.

YOUNG SOPHIE I'd give anything to have those hands.

SOPHIE But you see, you do have my hands. Look at them. The only difference is I've grown into mine – almost. And believe me, that's taken a while.

She holds YOUNG SOPHIE's hands.

SOPHIE These are beautiful hands. I think you look Splendid.

They hold hands. Big sister, little sister.

SOPHIE Right then. We'll both resolve to take good care of our bodies. Reasonable diet, plenty of exercise –

YOUNG SOPHIE Are you revving up for a big speech on the dangers of eating more than you should and then tossing it all in the loo?

SOPHIE . . . Yes.

YOUNG SOPHIE Did you ever do that?

SOPHIE No.

YOUNG SOPHIE Then Neither will I. That's settled.

SOPHIE *(Gives her a quizzical look.)* Right.

YOUNG SOPHIE Sometimes I hear Alice at night. Doing, you know. That. I feel so bad about it but I just can't bring myself to talk to her about it. It's so sad. She has everything going for her but she puts herself through hell. Forty lengths of the pool, every day, and hardly any food. And when she does eat, ohmygod.

SOPHIE Wolfing down her food at top speed?

YOUNG SOPHIE And so many of the girls do that! For the life of me, I don't under –

SOPHIE They're terrified.

YOUNG SOPHIE Sorry?

SOPHIE Last one, and all that. And it's true, it's something to avoid. Not that you should eat that way, but you can understand why no –

YOUNG SOPHIE But that's just it: I don't, I don't understand.

SOPHIE No one wants to be the last one at the table. Sitting alone.

YOUNG SOPHIE . . . That happens to me all the time.

An awkward moment between SOPHIES.

SOPHIE That was an incredibly silly thing to say. There's absolutely nothing wrong with being the last one sitting.

YOUNG SOPHIE Other than it marks you as odd or quirky –

SOPHIE No.

YOUNG SOPHIE Or stand-offish –

SOPHIE No!

YOUNG SOPHIE Or pathetic.

SOPHIE Absolutely not. That does not make you pathetic.

YOUNG SOPHIE Katherine says if you're going to talk with those people you'll never be P.L.U.

SOPHIE P.L. –

YOUNG SOPHIE People –

SOPHIE & **YOUNG SOPHIE** Like Us.

SOPHIE I knew that.

YOUNG SOPHIE That's her term. Horrid, isn't it. I would never use it.

SOPHIE I should hope not.

YOUNG SOPHIE But she's really sweet.

SOPHIE *(A whiff of a memory.)* Katherine.

YOUNG SOPHIE Until you get to know her, and then it's all that sort of hockey sticks, rah rah lifestyle the trendies adore. Plus she's gorgeous.

SOPHIE Right. And all of that would make her an expert on personal relations.

YOUNG SOPHIE No, all of that would make her a –

SOPHIE & **YOUNG SOPHIE** Cow.

YOUNG SOPHIE But the truth is, she goes down town, she has a boyfriend. None of that really matters, but it is a fact. And she does seem to get on so well with –

YOUNG SOPHIE *(Simultaneous.)* all the other trendies.

SOPHIE *(Simultaneous.)*
My mind screams out the truth,
while
My mouth smiles,
My head shakes,
My lips are still.

YOUNG SOPHIE Sorry?

SOPHIE Nothing, sorry. It's senility. My arty-farty mind is beginning to slip.

YOUNG SOPHIE Perhaps if I'd stop blathering.

SOPHIE Those people who walk alone, who eat alone. Those odd, quirky, interesting ones.

YOUNG SOPHIE Some of them.

SOPHIE Don't be scared to be friends with those people.

YOUNG SOPHIE I'm not. Usually.

SOPHIE Don't be scared to be one of those people.

YOUNG SOPHIE I try. Really, I do.

SOPHIE Well then, I admire your courage.

YOUNG SOPHIE *(To the presence/Audience.)* I'm sorry, I don't have a limitless supply of crisps. You'll just have to wait! Oh. I am sorry. *(To SOPHIE.)* He's worried that you're still cold.

SOPHIE He is?

YOUNG SOPHIE Yes, and he wonders if you he might offer you his coat. Though it's not what I would call a 'coat'. It's more of a cloak, wouldn't you say?

SOPHIE Oh, thanks ever so much, but –

YOUNG SOPHIE Of course, he's been carrying it around since 700 B.C. It is a bit tattered.

SOPHIE *(To the presence/Audience.)* It still looks splendid and thanks ever so much for the offer, but I'm fine, really. But thank you.

A moment.

YOUNG SOPHIE Do you actually see him, or are you just saying that for my benefit?

SOPHIE If I lie will you take away my crisp eating privileges?

YOUNG SOPHIE Yes.

SOPHIE You're not making this easy.

YOUNG SOPHIE Just the truth please. I'm quite serious.

SOPHIE . . . I don't actually see him. Not his physical presence. But I'm with him in spirit.

SFX: Another train passes. YOUNG SOPHIE opens another bag of crisps and offers some to SOPHIE. She accepts.

SOPHIE You know you're not the only one with an ancient poet for a confidante. I've been writing journal entries to mine for years.

YOUNG SOPHIE Journal entries? Does he write back?

SOPHIE Not that I know of. But he listens to all my poems. Always has – he has yet to complain.

YOUNG SOPHIE Yes, well mine gives me ideas for poems and stories. In my dreams. And he's a musician.

SOPHIE Mine's a musician. And he was banished to sea and later saved by a dolphin. And he never begs for crisps.

YOUNG SOPHIE You have me there.

SOPHIE But then I've never actually seen my confidante. Obviously you have a
better rapport.

YOUNG SOPHIE Probably because you don't offer him treats.

SOPHIE I'll have to try that sometime.

YOUNG SOPHIE Salt and vinegar. That's his favourite.

SOPHIE All these years I've been reciting to him. And writing. I never thought to offer him crisps.

YOUNG SOPHIE And you're quite sure you don't see him. My confidante.

SOPHIE *(Looks again.)* . . . No.

YOUNG SOPHIE Because I'd be happy to lend him to you. *(To the unseen presence.)* Is that all right? *(To SOPHIE.)* You can recite for him. I'm sure he'd like that. *(To the unseen presence.)* Sorry? *(To SOPHIE.)* He said yes.

SOPHIE Hmm.

YOUNG SOPHIE It was quiet but sincere.

SOPHIE Tell him –

YOUNG SOPHIE I'll warn you, he's a bit touchy.

SOPHIE I do appreciate the offer but no. Thank you.

YOUNG SOPHIE *(Looks to the unseen presence and shrugs her shoulders.)* You've hurt his feelings.

SOPHIE My God, can't you just toss him a crisp or bicky –

YOUNG SOPHIE He's waiting for you to recite something.

SOPHIE *(To the presence – annoyed:)* I JUST DON'T WANT TO. *(To YOUNG SOPHIE:)* Sorry. How rude was that? I'm sorry.

YOUNG SOPHIE It is a disappointment.

SOPHIE Right. Of course. *(To the presence:)* I'm sorry. *(To YOUNG SOPHIE:)* I don't suppose he knows when the next train will arrive.

YOUNG SOPHIE If he knows, he isn't telling.

SOPHIE Thought I'd ask.

SOPHIE surreptitiously looks again in search of the unseen presence. YOUNG SOPHIE catches the attempt.

YOUNG SOPHIE Thanks so much for letting me tell you about him. I wouldn't dream of sharing that information with any of my school friends. Or anyone else, really.

SOPHIE I'm honoured.

YOUNG SOPHIE They'd just think I'm a total loser.

SOPHIE No.

YOUNG SOPHIE They would. Some of them already do.

SOPHIE Ah, you mean some of those soulless, empty zombies. The ones who get excited about TV and shopping in Fellbridge.

YOUNG SOPHIE Emma Readhead and Co.

SOPHIE Readhead? I had a Emma Readhead in my class.

YOUNG SOPHIE Was she a soulless, empty zombie?

SOPHIE I'm afraid so. But the thing is –

YOUNG SOPHIE Yes?

SOPHIE They're not all mindless sheep, are they. It's really not as dismal as all that.

YOUNG SOPHIE No, of course not . . . Sometimes it's pretty dismal.

SOPHIE I was always homesick for a while, but don't you find it goes away.

YOUNG SOPHIE I've got to get into school mode. Then I'm fine.

SOPHIE Exactly. And it might take a while, it did for me, to find your niche – And don't say you won't, because you will; you'll establish yourself properly.

YOUNG SOPHIE If you say so.

SOPHIE Of course you'll have your little grumbles, don't we all, but I rather enjoy mine, strangely. Particularly when they're balanced with good things, and when really good things start to happen, I know I was so pleased because the year before *and* the year before that I went through a time of serious self-doubt when I thought perhaps I wasn't much good at anything. And then finally, finally I proved to people that I'm good at drama, which was so important because everyone had thought of me as not much good at anything and 'almost harmless'. And then people began to look *at* me instead of *through* me. And then one day, I remember the moment, I was sitting on my bed in my box . . . I'm sorry, I really am blathering.

YOUNG SOPHIE Please, I do need to hear this.

SOPHIE *(A bit puzzled.)* Right.

YOUNG SOPHIE You're sitting on your bed –

SOPHIE It's dark outside so I've drawn the curtain. Eric Clapton is playing quietly on my CD player and my room has that Saturday afternoon, faintly untidy look that accompanies me after I've been to town. And you know what? It dawns on me: I'm utterly happy. I am. With myself, my life, my darling parents, my brothers. I'm almost happy with my work. My friends, my box, my teachers. I'm doing pretty well here.

YOUNG SOPHIE And you wish you were back?

SOPHIE Oh God no. *(She laughs.)* I'm sorry. I shouldn't say that. I did love it there, by the end. But believe me, by the final term I was looking forward to getting away, to getting on with my life . . . such as it is.

SFX: a train in the distance.

SOPHIE *(She competes with the SFX of the train.)* Actually, things are going fine just now. They really are. Other than the fact my bank account is completely empty and I don't have the slightest clue where I am! Everything else is brilliant! brilliant, brilliant, brilliant!

A moment as the train passes. Without looking at one another, they both make the little drumming motion with the rhythm of the train.

SOPHIE I don't suppose you'd like to be a financial partner in a summer production of a new play. We're taking it to Edinburgh.

YOUNG SOPHIE Unfortunately, I'm not in a position to –

SOPHIE I'm joking, of course. About the finances. But I'm quite serious about doing some work experience with me, helping out with the show.

YOUNG SOPHIE I – thank you.

SOPHIE Then you'll consider it?

YOUNG SOPHIE I can't. I – I'm previously engaged.

SOPHIE Oh, gracious, well. If you're *Previously Engaged* –

YOUNG SOPHIE I'm afraid I am –

SOPHIE *(A playful interruption. Her next three lines are continuous.)* Of course you could help with costumes, props –

YOUNG SOPHIE I wish I could –

SOPHIE Have a fantastic time in Edinburgh, make an impact on the world –

YOUNG SOPHIE Sounds lovely –

SOPHIE Work with moi. You understand this is Edinburgh, my –

SOPHIE & **YOUNG SOPHIE** Mecca.

SOPHIE Exactly!

YOUNG SOPHIE I'd love to. Really. But I do have a prior commitment.

SOPHIE . . . Well then, if you decide to have a go at it, call me, will you? Or drop me a line. Have you got e-mail? Here, I've got a leaflet with all the numbers. *(Searching her pockets.)* I'm doing a bit of fundraising.

YOUNG SOPHIE Any luck with that?

SOPHIE No. *(Laughs.)* Well, a few pounds but we're just getting started. I can't seem to find my –

YOUNG SOPHIE You could just tell me your address.

SOPHIE *(Still searching for that leaflet.)* Odd. Right. 17 Sundial Court.

YOUNG SOPHIE Stonely, Middleton.

SOPHIE Would it be better to write that down?

YOUNG SOPHIE I won't forget.

SOPHIE MX20 4SJ; I could have sworn I had a stack of those in my pocket.

YOUNG SOPHIE You're directing then?

SOPHIE Director slash producer. Actually we've started a company.

YOUNG SOPHIE *(Impressed.)* A company.

SOPHIE Well, a small one.

YOUNG SOPHIE So you're going to be rich and famous? Cats on roller skates, that sort of thing?

SOPHIE gives her a withering look – strictly in fun.

YOUNG SOPHIE Silly question, sorry.

SOPHIE Someday, and this is something I've wished for for quite some time –

YOUNG SOPHIE I know what it is.

SOPHIE I don't see how you could.

YOUNG SOPHIE I don't see how anyone could spend ten minutes with you and not know.

SOPHIE It took me longer than that to give you the leaflet. *(Begins searching again.)* Not that I – what did I –

YOUNG SOPHIE That's not what I mean. It's a compliment, really.

SOPHIE Thank you! Then I suppose that's good, isn't it. I suppose that means – I'm living it.

YOUNG SOPHIE Your dream.

SOPHIE Well not the cold and penniless part, but everything else, mostly. Directing. Doing that one thing that's so special.

YOUNG SOPHIE It's quite lucky, that.

SOPHIE Oh yes. How many people get to freeze their bums off doing something they really love.

YOUNG SOPHIE Ever.

SOPHIE It's true though, isn't it. I mean really – what more could a girl wish for?

YOUNG SOPHIE Perhaps a date with some dreamy, gorgeous –

SOPHIE Well there's always that.

YOUNG SOPHIE Does it get better then? Do you fancy any boys?

SOPHIE I suppose there's one –

YOUNG SOPHIE I'm sorry, you don't have to –

SOPHIE I don't know if I fancy him particularly. I just find him really fascinating. He's an actor, so that's a bond. I think that's better than fancying someone, don't you? The problem though, we're totally inappropriate for each other and we always end up having a one- upmanship argument thingy, which he wins and that makes me cross. I'm always so rude to him. I wish I wasn't.

YOUNG SOPHIE That doesn't sound particularly romantic.

SOPHIE Exactly. Any sort of relationship would be a farce. So that's that. If I snogged him, he would go on an ego trip and I would get too emotionally involved. He'd humiliate me – or I him. And then I'd be miserable.

YOUNG SOPHIE It's sounding less and less romantic.

SOPHIE Yes, but then there's Robert and I suppose you could say, technically, I seem to be seeing him. Though it's a bit of a distance.

YOUNG SOPHIE Is he from Fellbridge?

SOPHIE Oh no, darling, Oxford.

YOUNG SOPHIE Oxford!

SOPHIE Yes, and he's so –

YOUNG SOPHIE *(In dreamland.)* Oxford.

SOPHIE Yes, with big blue eyes and one less 'A' than me at A level.

YOUNG SOPHIE Hurrah.

SOPHIE I know, perfect, isn't it.

YOUNG SOPHIE That's beyond perfect, that's –

SOPHIE Darling, it's perfect.

YOUNG SOPHIE Right.

SOPHIE And then there's Richard, who's terrific fun, a real giggle, but definitely not worth losing Robert for. Even though I think we may not be wholly compatible actually.

YOUNG SOPHIE With Richard?

SOPHIE Robert.

YOUNG SOPHIE Right.

SOPHIE Oh, do stop looking at me that way.

YOUNG SOPHIE *(Counting fingers – all in fun.)* Let's see then, that's one, two –

SOPHIE Darling, stop. I'm blushing.

YOUNG SOPHIE Of course you are.

SOPHIE And believe me, seriously, none of this is half as exciting as your first snog and all that sort of growing up thing. You're going to have a brilliant time of it.

SFX: another passing train. SOPHIE picks up the rhythm of the clickety-clack. YOUNG SOPHIE joins her.

As the sound dominates the stage, it's clear that the two SOPHIES are singing a duet – something along the lines of The Chordette's, 'Lollipop' (please include the finger-in-mouth 'pop').

. . . We hear the lyrics for a brief moment until another train passes. SOPHIE gets up to look for another incoming train . . . .

SOPHIE *(To no one in particular:)* WHERE ARE YOU?!

YOUNG SOPHIE Sorry?

SOPHIE This is soo bizarre. Annoying, isn't it?

YOUNG SOPHIE Sophie?

SOPHIE Sorry, I've just got to take a moment. I've got to suss it out.

YOUNG SOPHIE I should like to help if I could.

SOPHIE I was in the car. I was . . . driving the car.

YOUNG SOPHIE Are you all right, then?

SOPHIE Oh yes, yes. Chuffed as punch. Couldn't be better.

YOUNG SOPHIE Right.

SOPHIE Right.

A moment.

SOPHIE *(Most of the following is addressed to herself or the heavens.)* This is absolutely appalling. God. I was driving the car. I was . . . Here. I was . . . No one deserves it now, do they.
Did you hear me? WHAT DID I DO TO DESERVE THIS?!
WHERE's THE BLOODY TRAIN?!

A moment. No answer. To YOUNG SOPHIE:

Sorry. It's not you.

YOUNG SOPHIE bursts into tears. Covers her face.

Ohmygod. Sophie, please; you must believe that had nothing to do with you. That was entirely –

YOUNG SOPHIE *(Blows her nose.)* I've upset you.

SOPHIE No, in fact, Sophie: a friend of mine just told me, quite bluntly, he was sick of us bloody actors, always so demanding and prissy. And I told him to stop being his usual annoying self but he's right now, isn't he. I'm really sorry.

YOUNG SOPHIE *(One last nose blow.)* Is he the one you don't fancy? The fascinating one with the argument thingy?

SOPHIE laughs.

YOUNG SOPHIE I didn't mean it as a joke.

SOPHIE I think he was just trying to help me out of the abyss he thought I fell into when I didn't get into a certain University. And he needn't worry. I'm completely over it.

YOUNG SOPHIE Uh-huh.

SOPHIE Really. Carpe diem, and all that.

YOUNG SOPHIE Right.

SOPHIE I'm not bitter.

YOUNG SOPHIE Mm-hmn.

SOPHIE I feel fine about it all.

YOUNG SOPHIE Absolutely. I can tell by your face.

SOPHIE Tell by my –

YOUNG SOPHIE That's the face of someone who's –

SOPHIE Perfectly at peace.

YOUNG SOPHIE Right.

SOPHIE fails in her attempt to appear perfectly at peace.

YOUNG SOPHIE You didn't get into Oxford.

SOPHIE No. And that's it. No more chances. It's a failure I'll have to live with.

YOUNG SOPHIE It's not a failure.

SOPHIE It makes me wish I were going somewhere foreign, far away from the site of my shame.

YOUNG SOPHIE It must be very frustrating.

SOPHIE Yes.

An awkward moment.

SOPHIE It was the interview. They saw a mediocre loser, when I was, am, so fabulous. I still can't believe some of the shit I told them, and all the opportunities I had to shine and didn't. If I knew I had given it my best shot, and hadn't got in, I wouldn't mind so much. But I didn't. I gave it a pathetic, flustered, confused and half-hearted shot, and I'll never know whether I would have got in if I had given it my best. And that's the worst feeling. Now I'm consigned to the ranks of Oxford wannabes. When people ask if I got into Oxford, my family will have to say, "No, but she's going to Bristol" – and the people will say "ahh" and think to themselves uhuh, Oxford wannabe, less than Oxford.

YOUNG SOPHIE And when you stop to consider all the Oxbridge people. Imagine. To always be excluded.

SOPHIE I'm sorry –

YOUNG SOPHIE To be defined by this Forever. For Eternity.

SOPHIE I'm not quite sure I – follow you.

YOUNG SOPHIE Well think about it. Let's say God is a poet, and of course if there is a God you've got to think he's something of a poet, and then someone like, say, Shakespeare dies and floats up to the pearly gates but WHAM: no degree from Oxford! Didn't get in, *didn't get in!* Didn't even apply. Wouldn't have got in had he applied. You think they'll let him into heaven without that degree? Without so much as attending a single day. Go away sir! And take your buddy George Bernard What's-His-Name with you! I'm sorry, Mr. Keats. You, William Butler Yeats! Scoot along! Oxford does not approve. Nor can I. Application Rejected.

SOPHIE I somehow doubt Shaw or Keats are residing in heaven. Much less William Butler Yeats.

YOUNG SOPHIE My point exactly! And it's Just Not Fair.

SOPHIE takes a long look at YOUNG SOPHIE.

SOPHIE How old are you?

YOUNG SOPHIE Mrs. Huddleson says it's not too early to start in on the Oxbridge track and that I should plan on choosing sensible A level subjects to help me get in. And that means English and Religion are fine, but definitely not Theatre Studies. And I said – actually, I didn't say anything. I nodded my head and smiled but I thought, *Who gives a monkey's?* I don't care if I go to Oxford or Timbuktu; I want to study drama.

SOPHIE Exactly. That's – exactly –

YOUNG SOPHIE I'm lost without it. And even if I have no money, if I have to live in a tent. I'd be untrue to SOPHIE if I denied myself the chance to create drama.

SOPHIE That's essentially, not word for word, but that's what I said in the interview. I said I cannot not do it, if you know what I mean.

YOUNG SOPHIE Perhaps they were frightened by the double negative.

SOPHIE laughs.

YOUNG SOPHIE I think it sounds lyrical!

SOPHIE Right. We agree then? We'll do what we love despite the drawbacks.

YOUNG SOPHIE Absolutely.

SOPHIE Not that either one of us have much experience in the 'real world'. I shouldn't speak for you.

YOUNG SOPHIE The 'real world'. What's that?

SOPHIE There you have it. Maybe someday I'll settle down to English teaching or something.

YOUNG SOPHIE There's nothing wrong with that.

SOPHIE No, that's right. There's not. Some of my teachers were fantastic.

YOUNG SOPHIE Though it's not exactly –

SOPHIE The dream.

YOUNG SOPHIE & **SOPHIE** No.

YOUNG SOPHIE looks for something in her bag . . . .

YOUNG SOPHIE *(Offers a biscuit.)* Bicky?

SOPHIE Dear God, no.

YOUNG SOPHIE I was just –

SOPHIE Seriously, one more snack and I'll –

YOUNG SOPHIE Actually, I was offering one to –

SOPHIE Sorry. How rude is that? And I keep interrupting. Sorry.

YOUNG SOPHIE But you're welcome to have one. Arion says you're welcome to have his.

SOPHIE . . . I'm sorry?

YOUNG SOPHIE He said he doesn't want a biscuit. There's plenty if you'd like some.

SOPHIE Arion?

YOUNG SOPHIE My poet friend. If that's the word for it. "Confidante", I like that.

A moment.

SOPHIE I think I just need to move. Or walk or – be alone for a bit.

YOUNG SOPHIE You're not leaving? You don't have to meet him.

SOPHIE I know him. And. While I can't recall ever offering him a bicky, I'm well aware of who he was.

YOUNG SOPHIE Is.

SOPHIE Fine. "Is". *(Waves to the air.)* Hello Arion!

YOUNG SOPHIE I'm afraid you've scared him away.

SOPHIE Did I? Of course, how foolish of me. Then again, I'm not sure it's possible to scare him away seeing as he's *my ancient greek poet musician confidante.* Or was until you usurped him. And my Badger. And my – everything I can think of including, no doubt, my Bearings, which I really must find immediately and that's probably best done alone. Excuse me. I really must be moving on. Thanks ever so much for the jumper.

YOUNG SOPHIE Please keep it.

SOPHIE Lovely, thank you. And you're quite sure you'll be –

YOUNG SOPHIE I'm fine.

SOPHIE Somehow I'm sure you will be.

YOUNG SOPHIE *(Protective Badger snarl:)* Rrrrwowwll!

SOPHIE Right. Well then. Thanks again. Thank you ever so much.

SFX: train passing. SOPHIE gives a little wave goodbye. Exits.

YOUNG SOPHIE . . . She'll just be a minute or so. *(She bites into a biscuit.)* Would you like to – *(Touches her mouth.)* Sorry. *(Finishes chewing.)* Would you like to hear my new Haiku? I'm not sure they had those in 700 B.C., did they. Not in Greece anyway. Well what it is, it's a short poem with a deep meaning. Would you like to hear it? I don't suppose you have much choice, do you. Anyway, here it is:

> How can the End
> Be the Beginning again
> When All seems Lost?

Not bad, that. I'm just going to stop for a moment so you can think about it.

A brief moment. She takes another bite from the biscuit.

Have you thought about it? Because if you haven't, I can wait a bit longer . . . Actually, I can't. It means that when something dreadful happens, it seems the end, and yet it's the beginning of coping without, see?

SFX: Another train. SOPHIE enters, stands at a distance.

In fact, the more I think about it the more true it seems. Even in our blackest hours, there's always a chance to get better. There's no such thing as the end, only beginnings to take up and work on. I believe that, I really do.

The train passes . . . .

Sophie.

SOPHIE I'm totally knackered.

YOUNG SOPHIE I know.

SOPHIE I didn't come back for the train.

YOUNG SOPHIE Right.

SOPHIE Do you know what I see?

YOUNG SOPHIE I reckon I do.

SOPHIE It's more of a feeling, really. An awareness.

YOUNG SOPHIE A little glimpse of the present.

SOPHIE Of this moment. Of my place here. The thing is, it's all so . . . .

YOUNG SOPHIE Overwhelming.

SOPHIE Yes. I hear him laughing.

YOUNG SOPHIE And, unafraid.

SOPHIE I am alone.

YOUNG SOPHIE And.

A moment.

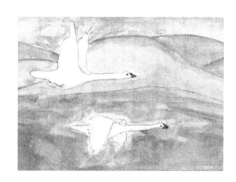

SOPHIE I look at the lights in the sky.
The clear moon,
Almost full, silver and remote.
And the present

YOUNG SOPHIE & SOPHIE Floods through me

In the off chance the production receives sponsorship from a fabulously wealthy corporation, please project a hologram of Arion here.

SOPHIE Washing away the loss.
And contentment, like wine
Smooth and clear and sweet,
Fills

SOPHIE & YOUNG SOPHIE My soul.

SOPHIE I look back and see
Myself beginning again,
And I say, as I follow you,
A long way behind:

YOUNG SOPHIE & SOPHIE "This is now".

YOUNG SOPHIE It is a comfort, isn't it.

SOPHIE The security of it all.

YOUNG SOPHIE In this strange grey town.
Blotted out by night.

SOPHIE Sophie.

YOUNG SOPHIE Deep voids of crowded air.
A flickering of neon sign.

SOPHIE Has he come for me?

YOUNG SOPHIE A deserted platform.
Across the other side,

SOPHIE Those are my words.

YOUNG SOPHIE On red benches –

SOPHIE *(A minor epiphany.)* No one sits.

YOUNG SOPHIE The box clock ticks, echoes
In the brimming space.

SOPHIE Flick.

YOUNG SOPHIE A minute passes.

SOPHIE People hurry to rain flecked cars
Enclosed in metal

YOUNG SOPHIE & **SOPHIE** Going home.

SOPHIE They see no stranger.

SOPHIE & **YOUNG SOPHIE** A barrier of space makes her
Untouchable.

YOUNG SOPHIE rises from the bench.

SOPHIE Yellow clouds.

YOUNG SOPHIE Blanket thick.

SOPHIE And trains, vast heaves
Of agonizing noise –

YOUNG SOPHIE reaches out – places an arm around SOPHIE's waist.

SOPHIE A flicker of faces,
Framed by black.
Flick flick swoosh
Gone.

SOPHIE & **YOUNG SOPHIE** Wind in her fingers.
The dark resignation hunches.
There are no trains stop here tonight.

A moment.

YOUNG SOPHIE It's time, Sophie.

SOPHIE Mm-hmn.

YOUNG SOPHIE Are you ready?

SOPHIE I believe so. Yes.

SFX: passing train. SOPHIE and YOUNG SOPHIE stand together for a moment. Fade to black.

End of Play

The End.....
or is it the beginning?

Sophie Large

BIOGRAPHICAL NOTES 1978 – 1998

SCHOOLS
The Carrdus School, Overthorpe Hall, Banbury;
Winchester House School, Brackley;
St. Swithun's School, Winchester.

DRAMA/ACTING
God in *Noyes Fludde*; Koong Se in *The Willow Pattern*;
Sarah Brown in *Guys and Dolls*; finalist in *Shakespeare
on the Platform*; Barbara Jackson in *Pack of Lies*;
Hesther Salomon in *Equus*; Meg Boyd in *Damn Yankees*;
Escalus in *Romeo and Juliet*, a National Youth Theatre
production.

DRAMA/DIRECTING
War on the Home Front written by Kate Bolwell,
co-directed with Sarah Copas; *Kindertransport* by
Diane Samuels; Artistic Director designate of
Pope-Afloat by Jon Groom, a Silver Lining Theatre
Company production.

SINGER
Chorus: *The Pearl Fishers*; Soprano, St. Swithun's
Senior Choir; Soprano soloist: *The Chichester Psalms*;
Soprano, The National Youth Choir of Great Britain.

POET
Senior Silver Medalist Award for Spoken Poetry,
The Poetry Society; author of *Innocence, Imagination,
A Sniff of the Real Me, Catkins, Sunglasses,
The Pleasant Scents of Spring, Catastrophically Speaking,
On Being Alone Outside on a Summer Night* and many
other poems.

WRITER
Author of many stories, diaries, letters, plays, etc.

TEACHER
Drama workshop teacher at The Carrdus School
during gap year.

The end is the beginning . . . Sophie's Haiku

The life of our beloved daughter Sophie came to an abrupt end on February 10th, 1998, when the car she was driving was involved in an accident. She was nineteen and currently absorbed with planning a production of a friend's play which she hoped would premiere at the Edinburgh Festival Fringe that summer.

Shattered by our loss, we were determined to heed the wisdom of Sophie's own Haiku:

How can the End
Be the Beginning Again
When All Seems Lost?

We established a charity, Sophie's Silver Lining Fund, to help young people struggling to finance their training in acting or singing. Many people give us generous donations and we have embarked on a variety of successful fund-raising projects. To date we have given or promised financial help to the value of nearly £40,000, assisting students from all over world to study at leading drama schools and conservatoires, mainly, but not exclusively, in Britain.

One of these fund-raising ideas was to publish a collection of Sophie's own writing, which we entitled "Sophie's Log – Thoughts and feelings in poetry and prose". Thousands of copies of this book have been sold all over the world. Many people are deeply moved and impressed with the charm, wisdom and beauty of Sophie's writing. The money we raise from sales of this book represents a most significant part of our charity's income.

Sophie's Log is now being used widely as a resource by school teachers to encourage both creative writing and emotional literacy. A Scheme of Work to help teachers can be downloaded from our charity website. This enables students to follow Sophie's example in writing freely about their own thoughts and feelings. We hope to promote this educational aspect of the book in the future, when we have secured further sponsorship. The play "Sophie" is part and parcel of this valuable educational resource.

In 2001 it was one of our very first sponsored students, Erin Hurme, from the USA, that introduced Bryan Willis to us.-She was studying acting at the prestigious Guildhall School of Music and Drama in London. We wanted to commission a playwright to create a short play around the person of Sophie herself. (This was partly because we wished such a play to have its world premiere at the Edinburgh Festival Fringe. This did happen in 2002, the play receiving very good reviews, including the precious four stars from The Scotsman. "A definite must-see.")

The resulting play by Bryan Willis, simply entitled "Sophie", derives much of its content from Sophie's Log as well as from other sources of her writing. In researching the play he also interviewed many of her friends and family.

We are pleased that the British Broadcasting Corporation has since commissioned Bryan Willis' play "Sophie" as a radio play. This will be broadcast as the afternoon play on BBC Radio Four on April 10th 2004. This speaks volumes about the quality and the universal appeal of Bryan's play.

We encourage retiring audiences and readers that have enjoyed this play to buy a copy of Sophie's Log. This way our charity can continue to assist impecunious and talented students who, just like Sophie, want to study drama or singing.

CHERRY & STEPHEN LARGE
Sophie's parents and founders of Sophie's Silver Lining Fund

www.silverlining.org.uk

Sophie's Log – thoughts and feelings in poetry and prose by Sophie Large.
ISBN 0-9534901-0-6 from Ottakar's Bookshop in England. Tel: +44 (0) 1295 270498.
44 *Or from www.wheesh.com*